THE GREATEST HERO

Jesus is exactly who the Bible truthfully says he is: the rightful king over everything and the true hero of this world.

If true, then Jesus *is* a big deal. And he's a big deal that confronts your life.

We usually live with ourself as our king—"No one tells me what to do!" And we all live with ourself as our hero—"I can handle this!"

How's that working out for you?

If we're honest, don't we all end up needing help? We need someone who has the power to rescue us from the evil around us—and even the evil inside us.

But Jesus did more than make incredible statements about who he was. He also gave lots of brilliant teaching (Matthew 5–7; 10; 13; 18; 23–25). People were amazed by what he taught (Matthew 7:28–29; Mark 6:1–6). When the Bible experts of his day tried to trick Jesus, he stumped them with wise and logical answers (Matthew 22:15–46).

No, Jesus wasn't insane. He was a genius. So Option 2 isn't an option either. And that leaves us with one final answer.

Option 3: Jesus Is King

Who is Jesus? He's not a liar. He's not a lunatic. (And he's also not a legend dreamed up by the disciples.) Instead, Jesus is exactly who the Bible truthfully says he is: the rightful king over everything and the true hero of this world.

Have you ever noticed how often books and movies tell stories about heroes who defeat evil and save the world?

Think about Superman. He comes into the world as a baby, and when he grows up, although he looks like a normal human, he uses all his power to rid the world of evil.

Think about Anna from *Frozen*. She sacrifices her own life—even for people who don't deserve it. As a result, her love brings the warmth of life to a frozen world.

And think about Frodo from *The Lord of the Rings*. He left his home to go on an adventure, and in great weakness carries the burden of evil, even if it kills him. Why? To save the world.

It's like we humans write these stories because deep down, we all know what we really need. The human race needs someone—to help us, love us, and rescue us.

Someone like Jesus.

Really? "Someone like Jesus"? How do superheroes point to Jesus?

The Bible teaches that Jesus came to earth to clean up and conquer the evil that had spread throughout the world and corrupted human life.

Don't just take my word for it. You should meet Jesus by listening to his own words. But prepare yourself: He made some pretty intense statements.

Jesus declared he could give people true life (John 5:21–29; 6:35). Jesus told people that he could forgive sins (Mark 2:1–12; Luke 7:48–49). And Jesus even claimed to have the authority of God (Matthew 28:18; John 17:2).

What kind of person would make these kinds of huge claims?

According to C. S. Lewis (author of *The Chronicles of Narnia*), you've basically got three options.

Option 1: Jesus Is Lying

Think about the strong statements that Jesus made about himself. Anyone could *say* that he had all authority. Anyone could just *tell* people that he could give them true life or forgiveness. But he'd be lying.

Yet Jesus did more than merely talk. He calmed storms—something only God can do (Mark 4:35–41). He healed people that no one else could help (Mark 5:1–20). And he raised people from the dead (Mark 5:21–43). Jesus proved his words with his actions! So Option 1 isn't really an option.

Option 2: Jesus Is Insane

Some people might say that Jesus wasn't lying but that he went around making wild statements. The world is full of crazy people. What if Jesus meant well but was actually out of his mind?

But if Jesus is the true hero and king over the whole world, how are you going to respond?

You may be thinking, "I want to believe in Jesus and follow him, but I don't know how." I've got good news: All it takes is believing with your heart and saying so with your mouth. If you want to give your life to King Jesus right now, you can do it. Consider praying something like this:

> *Heavenly Father, I believe that Jesus Christ is your Son and that he died on the cross to save me from my sin. I believe that he rose again to life and that he invites me to live forever with him in heaven as part of your family. Because of what Jesus has done, I ask you to forgive me of my sin and give me eternal life. Please guide me to a Bible-believing church where I can grow as a Christian with others who love Jesus. Amen.*

The Greatest Hero

Young people look up to superheroes, but do they know that the greatest hero of all isn't a fictional character? This tract for middle schoolers explains who Jesus is and how he came to rescue them.

Learn More

To browse more tract themes and accessories, visit crossway.org/evangelism-resources. To place an order, email sales@crossway.org or call 1 (800) 872-2871.

PACKAGE CONTAINS 25 TRACTS

CROSSWAY
crossway.org

9 781682 164457
CHILDREN & YOUTH